SECRETS

to an

ENCOUNTER

with

GOD

Joshua Giles

84 how people miss their encounters
84 PURSUE GOD CHASE AFTER HIM
87 2 PURGE OUR SPIRIT
89 we must make ourselves available
only if we are willing to pay the price
72 JESUS HAD BREAKTHRU AFTER BREAKTHRU
A BIPRODUCT OF SOLITUDE / TIMES of SEPARATION
ISOLATING HIMSELF TO PRAY
74 We too must SEPARATE OURSELVES & HIDE IN GOD
96 W/C
86 FASTING AFFECTS the CELLS & FLUSHES OUT TOXINS
& REJUVENATES SEEKING GOD

Secrets to an Encounter with God
Copyright © 2019 by Joshua Giles

80) had 1 LONEN 2 PERMITS ALL NEEDS
& completely set them aside   I dedicated

Reference: 1. Intercession. 2. Fasting. 3. Prayer Life.

100 % of my time I seek the LORD

72: A TIME OF SEPARATION FROM THE WORLD
3 1/2 YRS OF PRAYER & FASTING N SEPARATION: HIDING
IN GOD

CONTENTS

DEDICATION

I WOULD LIKE TO DEDICATE MY FIRST BOOK OF many to come to God, my Father, Jesus, my Lord and the Holy Spirit, my Comforter; along with my lovely wife, Dieuta, who has stood my side for more than a decade at the time of this publication. Her spirit of worship has contributed to many of my encounters with God.

I also dedicate this book to my two children, Isaiah and Isabelle, who will carry my legacy to another generation.

Josh

INTRODUCTION

SOMEONE MAY ASK THE QUESTION, IS IT STILL possible to have an encounter with God. The answer is yes. Throughout the Bible, many of God's servants had encounters with God; i.e., Abraham, Moses, Jacob, and Paul; as well as individuals throughout church history; i.e., Augustine, Martin Luther, Kathryn Kuhlman and Billy Graham, just to name a few.

Do you long for a genuine "God encounter" in your life? Do you wonder whether or not such experiences still happen today? Do you wonder if it could happen to you? Take heart. God encounters do happen and not just to "super-Christians".

This book is for those who are hungry for more of God. Unfortunately, some Christians are satisfied with just going to church and praying before their meals. That's the difference between religion and relationships.

God never intended for us to be religious but to have an intimate relationship with the living God.

In this book, *Secrets to an Encounter with God*, I share my story that begins with my passion to become a Major League baseball player to my pursuit after God. My experience is not extraordinary but there are secrets to having an extraordinary relationship with God. By combining certain aspects of worship, meditation, fasting, and prayer, I am personally convinced that there are levels of dimensions in the spirit realm that can be a part of every believer's walk with God. Many Christians may have a passion to experience an encounter, but few are willing to pay the price. However, there are no short cuts to experiencing a heavenly encounter.

Winning the battle of the mind, crucifying the flesh, and developing certain spiritual disciplines can unlock the doors to another realm. Discover the secrets to an encounter with God and realize the full potential for the life of a believer.

Joshua Giles

1

THE CURVEBALL

Many are the plans in a person's heart,
but it's the LORD'S purpose that prevails.

(Proverbs 19:21, NIV)

SINCE CHILDHOOD, MY DREAM WAS TO play professional baseball. I was willing to train, practice, and place all my efforts for this lifetime goal. In high school and college, I was a pitcher and I was a good at it, too. Others around me recognized I had a gift and it led me to believe that, one day, I would be playing in the majors. Like most any other sport, only the elite make it. Little did I know, in my journey, I would open myself to things that influenced my life negatively.

When we associate ourselves with the wrong crowd, we end up opening doors to spirits. Intentional or not, we make alignments with the enemy making a way for demonic infiltrations. People, especially young persons, have no clue that the decisions he or she makes have a direct impact on their destiny. Most Christians are oblivious to the effects of soul ties (ungodly connections).

I was with the wrong crowd; involved with high-level gang members, drug dealers and bad people in general. So, naturally, I loved listening to rap music like most other kids; although, I had no clue I was allowing demons into my life.

In my college years, I stayed with my dad in South Carolina. One night, the spiritual realm became more real than ever before. It's like when you look at the blinds in a window, even though they are very thin, they block our view to the outside. When the blinds are opened, we can see the other side. In the spirit realm, there is a thin layer between the natural and the supernatural; and it makes us significantly more sensitive to the unseen world.

That night, God decided to open the spiritual "blinds" and I began to see demons all over the place. I was not sleeping. I was wide-awake and I could identify them. My level of perception was unusual. I could feel things around me like when someone is beside you. I knew when spirits were nearby. I knew when they were outside walking around my property. I was terrified to sleep or to get up in the middle of the night to use the bathroom. I would usually wait until the sun rose before I felt comfortable enough to get out of bed.

This was not something I was used to nor had anyone taught me how to respond when this kind of thing happens. I thought, at times, I was going crazy. But God was opening my eyes to see what I had allowed into my life. I was raised to believe in God. I went to church. However, I never had a personal relationship with God. I was not exposed to the power of God or the supernatural. Everything was religious, dead spiritually, and it prevented me from having any kind of true relationship with the living God. My parents did not know anything about the supernatural either.

In the middle of the night, the spirits tormented me. One night, it was so bad I called my dad and asked him to come and pray for me. He did not understand what was going on. It was new to him too. Nevertheless, he laid his hands on me and said a quick prayer.

On another occasion, I cried out, "I'm not dealing with this anymore God. Either kill me or deliver me." Obviously, God decided to deliver me. But how He chose to do it would change my life forever. God has a way of reaching us right where we are and He reached me on the baseball field.

In baseball and softball, the curveball is a type of pitch thrown with a characteristic grip and hand movement that imparts forward spine to the ball, causing it to dive as it approaches the plate.[1] It is thrown slower and with more overall break than a slider, and it is used to keep hitters off-balance. When executed correctly by a pitcher, a batter expecting a fastball will swing too early and over the top of the curveball.[2]

I had a plan for my life—baseball. But God had a plan too, and when I thought everything was going

---

[1] https://en.wikipedia.org/wiki/Curveball
[2] http://m.mlb.com/glossary/pitch-types/curveball

my way and my future was set in stone, God threw me a curveball.

Twelve hours after I told God to deliver me or kill me, I had a college baseball game. I was exhausted. Part of the pregame routine is taking batting practice. I was a pitcher so, my job was to be in the outfield catching balls. Then, one of the players from the other team walked up to me and we greeted one another.

He said, "The spirit of God is strong on me right now. I see that you had a car wreck a few years ago. The devil tried to kill you. Your grandmother and your family were praying for you. And you're being tormented at night by demons."

When I heard that, my heart stopped. I thought, *what in the world is going on? How could this kid, who has never met me before in my life, come over here and tell me that I had a car wreck a few years ago?*

I hit a person head-on going 80 miles an hour. The accident was so bad I did not get to play my senior year.

The player asked if he could pray for me. I said, "Yes, of course." Even though it seemed embarrassing, I did not expect him to do anything, except say a quiet prayer. But no, he laid his hands on me and when he did, I could feel the power of God. When he finished, I went to my dugout and the only thing running through my mind was that God was calling me into ministry. I could no longer focus on the game. I could only think, God was answering my prayer.

When the game was over, I ran to the opposing team's bus. The young man who prayed for me told me that he served with a minister who was from

Africa, who was conducting crusades. The player gave me his number so I could remain in contact with him. He also gave me a piece of paper that contained a prayer entitled, "Thunder Prayers." I thought, *what in the world is thunder prayer?*

Later, I started reading the thunder prayer, and when I did, the power of God was so strong. These were prayers I have never heard of before, prayers using the name of Jesus, and renouncing demonic strongholds that were operating against my mind. I was in awe. I had to call my dad to tell him what just happened.

When I got home, I showed him the thunder prayers. That night, he read it, and it touched his life as well. When my dad went to work, he made copies of the prayer, and gave them to everyone.

Three or four weeks went by before I contacted the young man from the baseball game. I wanted to know more. I could not get enough. We became friends and he was pleased to hear how hungry I was to learn more of the things of the spirit. He invited me to a crusade in Georgia, where the evangelist from of Africa would minister.

About five days before the event was to take place, I came home from a church service extremely exhausted. Something felt odd, but I just thought I was tired. I did not know that it was spiritual. I went to lie down and the moment I did, the hand of the Lord came upon me—a hand of God bigger than my body. Suddenly, God picked me up by my neck, and pulled me out of my body and carried me in the realm of the spirit. I felt like a little puppy being carried by its neck. Then, God dropped me at a specific location and immediately the fire of God was all over me. I looked at my body and there were flames all over me. I felt the burning power of the Lord.

Suddenly, I was in a dark room. I could see what looked like a witch in the distance. I screamed out, "What are you doing here"?

"You know why I'm here!" she replied.

When she responded back to my question, fear overtook me. Immediately, the fire went out and the power left me. I felt naked without God's presence, without His fire. But the hand of God was behind me, pushing me down the hallway to confront her. I resisted, but just when I was about to face her, God picked me up and transported me back. When He dropped me in my body, I came to my senses. It was like a bad dream, even though it was not a dream.

When we first encounter something at this level, in the spirit realm, it will blow our mind. We want to tell everybody. But, whom would we tell? Who would believe us? The Bible declares in the book of

Revelation that John was taken in the spirit, so obviously something like this can happen.

I learned from that experience the Lord was showing me that whenever we battle things in the realm of the spirit, we must have complete confidence that Christ is *with* us and *in* us. We cannot be afraid, because satan is a master illusionist. He is a master at deception. He is a master at fear.

Since it was my first experience, I did not win that battle. It was a learning experience of what happens when God takes us into another dimension—deeper into encounters that becomes our spiritual résumé. In order to walk in authority, we have to be tested. We are tested not only in the natural, but in the supernatural.

When Jesus was tested in the wilderness, He was there with wild animals and was tested by the devil.

However, the Bible says when Jesus came out of the wilderness; He came out in the power of the spirit.

God taught me that we always have to engage in the spirit realm. We have to be the one to initiate the action. We should never take a step back. We need to be the crazy lunatic in the realm of the spirit. The enemy trembles when he sees us, because he knows that the power of God is within us.

He will do everything in his power to make himself look bigger, stronger, faster, and scarier; anything he can to knock us off the rhythm of faith. The Bible says *"the wicked flee though no one pursues, but the righteous are as bold as a lion,"* (Prov. 28:1, NIV). A lion is fierce. A lion attacks. A lion jumps at its prey.

I learned to fight my lions, to fight my bears, to fight my Goliaths, and to fight my Saul's, just as David had to face his lion, his bear, his giant, and his opposition. These are representations of what believers, who carry a high level of authority, will go through in order to possess that level of kingship and authority in the realm of the spirit. This encounter happened just one week before going to a crusade in Georgia.

On my way to the crusade, I got lost. I was so mad. I started cussing because I knew I was going to be late. However, when I finally arrived, this man from Africa, a minister I had never seen before in my life, was already preaching—preaching with such authority, like something I had never experienced before.

At the end of his sermon, he said, "Lift your hands." And when I did, I felt a physical wind hit me. I suddenly started laughing—almost uncontrollably. I remember thinking, *what am I doing. Am I drunk?* I was laughing in church, and this was not normal, at least not for me. Even though I grew up in the Bible belt, I had never seen or experienced anything like this.

I had to excuse myself. Even though I felt good, it was as if I was being disrespectful for laughing during a church service. I did not know that it was biblical. It was an expression of the spirit, of joy, or the Holy Ghost laughter. I had never experienced that before, but it was awesome. I was grinning from ear to ear. I never felt joy like that in my life.

Then the minister said, "Anybody that's been afflicted in your mind, I want you to come forward for prayer."

I had been tormented in my mind for years. It is part of my family, as there is a lot of iniquity and suicide in my family history. My mind was consistently attacked. I could never control my thoughts. I would experience outbursts of rage and anger.

I was standing in line for prayer, and this evangelist came up to me, laid his hands on me, and I literally felt like the weight of a piano lifted off my back. I felt so free, so light that, I felt like I could float through the ceiling.

When the service was over, I saw the young man from the baseball game. He asked me if I would like to meet the preacher. When we approached the minister, I could see that he had eyes of fire like something I had never seen before. Afterwards, we had a meal together, and then he called someone on the phone from another country and the two were speaking in an African dialect. Oddly, he handed me the phone. Little did I know there was a prophet on the other end who was discerning things about me.

I handed the phone back and the minister asked me to come to Florida with him. I left during my third-year of college, leaving my baseball scholarship behind. I was going to Florida to travel with a man who I did not know and I figured everyone would think I was crazy.

When we walk in the anointing, we walk in our destiny and at that level, we can be misunderstood. However, I was convinced that God would begin to redeem, restore, deliver, and open my family to my decision, and eventually that is what happened.

I moved to Florida, not sure what would come of it, but it was the greatest training ground and a spiritual boot camp. I began to walk in a realm of the spirit that was so powerful and this is where I started learning secrets to an encounter with God.

2

FASTING

"Even now," declares the Lord, "return to me with all your heart, with fasting and weeping and mourning."

(Joel 2:12, NIV)

FASTING IS THE WILLING ABSTINENCE OR reduction from some or all food, drink or both, for a period of time. An absolute fast or dry fasting is normally defined as abstinence from all food and liquid for a defined period. Other fasts may be partial, restrictive, limiting only particular foods or substances, or be intermittent.[1] Fasting is recommended by nutritionists and some doctors.

---

[1] https://en.wikipedia.org/wiki/Fasting

But the Bible suggests that fasting should be combined with prayer and meditation.

The combination of fasting and prayer is not to be a ritual or routine for religious purposes. Fasting and praying is not useful if it is a human-engineered method or plan. Nor are they to be a means to manipulate God to act on our behalf because of a trial or tribulation. Rather, fasting and praying are Bible-based disciplines that are appropriate for all believers of all ages, throughout all centuries, in all parts of the world.

I was surprised to learn that many people in the church have never been taught about fasting and prayer, and many have, therefore, never done so. As a result, they do not know why fasting and praying are important, or what the Bible teaches about it, its benefits, purpose, or what works best for those who wish to go on a fast.

I am convinced that in order to be in God's presence, this is one of the secrets to have an encounter. Fasting is not something that we do on occasion—it has to become a lifestyle. When I say we must fast, I don't mean fasting TV or social media. God has ordained a method for biblical fasting and it defines its purpose for doing so.

The first example is found in Matthew chapter 9:14-15.:

"One day the disciples of John the Baptist came to Jesus and asked him, "Why don't your disciples fast like we do and the Pharisees do?"

"Jesus replied, 'Do wedding guests mourn while celebrating with the groom? Of course not. But someday the groom will be taken away from them and then they will fast."

This passage describes the Jewish custom of that day in regards to preventing a marriage from being cursed or a sign of "bad luck." It was inappropriate for a person to be in the presence of a bride or groom and appear sad or gloomy. It was also their tradition for a person whom fasted to wear dingy clothes and cover their face with ash or dirt as a sign of desperation or sorrow.

Our Lord's response reveals that, for a time, the groom [Jesus] was celebrating with His disciples. But soon, the wedding [His presence] would be over and at that time, His disciples would fast. Neither John's disciples nor the Pharisees were in His presence on a daily basis, so they were not in the same category as The Twelve. A day was coming when the disciples would fast.

Fasting keeps the flesh in check. Fasting will disconnect you from anything that hinders us from tapping into the presence of God. If we desire His presence and have never fasted we are missing out on a secret ingredient that provides focus and insight to the things of the spirit realm.

When I meet people, who say they are hungry for God, I can gauge their spiritual life when I ask how much they fast. I'll ask someone, "How's your lifestyle of fasting or how much do you fast"? Some say, "I try to fast, you know, once every few months." Or someone will say, "Well, I haven't fasted in a year or two." It is impossible for us to function at the level God has intended for us to function if we are not maintaining a lifestyle of fasting.

In today's society, there's so much filth and defilement; so many ways the enemy leeches on to us. When we think of a leech and how it can latch on to us and suck blood, it is the same way with the enemy, but in a deceptive manner. We don't even know it is happening. Fasting will put us in a state of high-level perception where nothing can get past our radar. Not only will nothing get past our radar, but you will get closer to the Lord.

If we do not consistently fast, our discernment is not on point. We cannot know how to interpret a dream, or how to deal with a spiritual attack. We can go about our daily lives not knowing that the enemy has entered our soul.

The enemy can come in and sow tares among the good things in our life. When I have bad dreams, I know the level of the dream requires a specific level of fasting to break the power of the enemy off my life or to break an assignment.

Every day we have to walk in the spirit and if we want to walk at the level God has called us, demonic encounters in our dreams will weaken our spiritual antenna. It will weaken our prayer life. It will weaken our connection with the Lord. Can we function with these bad dreams even if we don't fast? Yes, but our impact and everything about our spiritual life becomes diluted, it will affect all areas.

God wants us to operate at a level 10 but because we have neglected to deal with the tares the enemy is sowing in our life, we might only be functioning at level six. The enemy wants to put out the fire. The enemy wants to cause our light to be dim. We must fast and pray in order to come out of that situation quickly.

There are too many people that want to play the game of Christianity but never want to pay the price to operate at that level or dimension of authority. Fasting breaks off bondage. It destroys yokes. Fasting clears up our perception. It sharpens our discernment. It opens our spiritual ears and eyes. It begins to take us deeper in the realm of the spirit like nothing else can.

One of the things I learned about when God was teaching me in the area of fasting was in my spiritual hunger. The moment I tasted the goodness of the Lord through encounters, I started seeing the supernatural. It became real to me. It was like a whole other world that most Christians have no clue about. So many believers miss out on understanding the spiritual realm. That is sad because we have all been given access through the blood of Christ.

Too many are bound with religion and put God in a box. Unfortunately, some are like a religious Pharisee, which is one of the reasons why most people cannot function in the Body of Christ. When people look at the church service, they have no desire to go in because what they are seeing, most of the time, is spiritually dead. Why would someone want to go somewhere that is dead? We are supposed to go to church and feel life, the presence of the Lord and the love of Christ. Not into a place where it is boring. God is not boring!

When I started fasting, I had no clue what I was getting into, but I knew I was feeling something incredible. God imparted His life so I could experience new levels of love, joy, and wisdom. Even my IQ increased! Now that sounds crazy to say, but yes, as I begin to fast, I actually got smarter.

When I was a child, they said I had attention deficit disorder. They labeled me with all kinds of issues, but when they saw me on the baseball field, it was a different story. I could concentrate and dominate as one of the best players in the nation. They said if he can concentrate there, he can concentrate in the classroom. The thing is, I hated putting my effort into the things that were not enjoyable.

When I began to fast, I had clarity of mind. My ability to articulate and solve problems became much easier. I was surprised that I not only increased in spiritual wisdom and revelation, but my physical conditions improved as well.

While living in Florida, I was a celebrity trainer and was considered one of the top trainers in all of Major League baseball. When it comes to specializing in body training for athletes, I'm known as an expert. So taking the perspective of what I know in the natural world and what fasting does, how it affects the cells and flushes out toxins, it can rejuvenate in a way that nothing else can.

But one of the reasons why it is hard for most believers to fast is because they feed their flesh too much. I don't mean with physical food. I mean their flesh is so strong so they don't feel the need to desire the things of God. We have to make a choice to follow the Lord and do what we know the Lord is leading us to do, even when we don't feel it. We must force it until we love it.

The reason we have to force it, at first, is because we are dealing with the flesh. We constantly face two battles that are raging here on earth, the empowerment of the flesh and sin. The flesh is always craving sinful desires because of what happened with Adam and Eve. The sinful nature and the temptations with the lust of the flesh do not go away completely until we are in glory.

We are not perfect. We were born into sin, so a sinful nature always wants to pull away from the things of God. When we feed our flesh our spirit man begins to lose power. It is like weighing a balance beam. Whichever one we feed the most is the one we serve. We have to force ourselves to read the Bible. We have to force ourselves to praise and worship. We have to force ourselves to fast and pray. We have empowered the flesh for so long that we have to change the balance structure. When we do and the Lord becomes more real, your flesh is crucified at a different level.

Our spirit man begins to arise and we begin to feel the presence of God. We encounter the supernatural, and then, the balance shifts and the love for the spiritual things increases—love, peace, joy, and the love for our neighbor starts to appear.

3

SETTING THE ATMOSPHERE

Surely the righteous shall give thanks to Your name; The upright shall dwell in Your presence.

(Psalm 140:13, NKJV)

ONE OF THE THINGS THAT GOD BEGAN to teach me in order to have an encounter with Him was how important it is to *set the atmosphere*. One of my favorite things that I tell people all the times is, when it comes to entering into the presence of God and going into the supernatural, extracting what we need, we have to learn that it is all about atmosphere!

An atmosphere is the pervading tone or mood of a place, situation, or work of art. One source says an atmosphere is "a particular environment or surrounding influence."[1] Obviously, this is not the only definition found in the dictionary, however, the atmosphere that I am referring to is a particular environment – the driving force or influence that has a direct affect upon a society or culture. Throughout history, music and the arts has had a huge impact upon culture.

In the 60s and 70s, America experienced one of the greatest cultural shifts in history. A movement that began announcing peace, love and rock-n-roll empowered a generation of young people in the midst of the civil rights movement and the Vietnam War. Elvis, Woodstock, and the Beatles, just to name

---

[1] https://www.vocabulary.com/dictionary/atmosphere

a few, created a new outlook on life, one with new hairstyles, radical changes in clothing and PDA "public displays of affection" on TV, the movies and in society itself.

The Hippie Movement was an ambiance that sustained and created a culture that would eventually be the catalyst for a radical paradigm shift in American society. An atmosphere sustains everything. Therefore, if we want to establish a culture of Christ, the supernatural, we must sustain an atmosphere.

As I wrote in chapter two, the Lord began to move upon me in the spirit. I needed to set an atmosphere when I went into a fast. Not that I needed to do it during a fast; I just needed to learn the value of fasting. I needed to learn what fasting could do to create an atmosphere to be in God's presence.

3 CD

Before iTunes or iPhones were common, I attained three CD players and placed them in different rooms in my house. One CD player had the Bible, one had warfare prayer and one had worship. I played them every day on repeat 24/7.

Now you may be thinking, how loud were you playing them? Weren't they distracting? They weren't playing loud, but rather at a level that we could still have day-to-day activity without being disrupted or without creating confusion. It played loud enough to create atmosphere. So, prayer, the Bible, and worship were going forth. When you're sustaining an atmosphere like that, it attracts angelic activity and the presence of God.

Sustaining an atmosphere while we are at home watching TV, playing outside, cooking, or whatever, created an environment that was welcoming to the Holy Spirit. The power of God was consistently there. This was a time when I encountered the supernatural on a nightly basis and when it started

happening it blew my mind. *3CD's ONE! WARFARE PRAYER / CRY, WORSHIP / ONT: The BIBLE*

As I applied these three sounds, it created an

energetic atmosphere and was the key reason why I

was able to experience God at a new level. We would

be sitting on the couch and feel the presence of God

and before we knew it, we would be worshiping,

reading the Bible or praying. It was a constant

saturating environment.

Now with that said, it also brought great

opposition. Do not let that scare you. Fear is not of

God. We should never allow the enemy to intimidate

us. The enemy recognizes shifts in the spirit realm.

You see, when he looks at us in the spiritual realm,

he sees light. He sees fire. He sees angelic activity.

We have a clear example of this in the Bible with

Jacob's ladder. It was an open portal and the angels

ascended and descended—angelic activity transpire-

ing from the heavens and the earth.

When the enemy looks at us and we are about to give birth to a blessing of God, the light (spiritual energy) around us intensifies. It gets brighter and the fire around us intensifies. The angelic activity increases. So, what the enemy says is, "Man, I don't know what is happening with Joshua over there, but we have to find a way to stop it"! The enemy does not know what is going on—he is not omniscient (all knowing). Nevertheless, he can see that something is happening in the spiritual realm around us.

It might be a spiritual download that's transpiring. It might be a breakthrough or a miracle about to manifest in our lives. When this happens, demonic forces realize that they must attack before it is too late. They want to stop our breakthrough, our miracle, or our spiritual deposit. They do not know what is going on because they cannot break the God barrier.

Because of the illuminate light, the enemy first searches for an open door, hoping to find iniquity in the soul, because iniquity is the easiest way for satan to enter into someone's life. In order to entrap us, the enemy searches for iniquity—the sins of the ancestors, which is the bloodline—the easiest way to bring someone down or get off track. They attempt to find out what is in our bloodline and try to tempt us in that area.

Even doctors recognize iniquity. The medical field does not call it iniquity; they call it hereditary. They will ask, "Has anyone in your family had cancer"? They ask questions because they understand that hereditary diseases and situations can be passed down from generation to generation through the bloodline. So, when the enemy is looking at us, they search on a "spiritual computer" in the realm of the spirit, looking for a stronghold, a dysfunction, or a particular repetitive sin in our bloodline to gain access. It may be with alcoholism, sexual sin, or some other addiction that has plagued our family for years.

We may be in a situation at work, for instance, one of our coworkers offers us to go out for a drink, and then we have to make a choice. If alcoholism was in our bloodline or it is something we struggled with in the past, we have to make a decision on how we will respond. The enemy can creep into our life. If we make the wrong choice, we can open the door to the devil. He comes in and infiltrates our bubble. He gains access to our system because we allow him to come in.

The Bible says in Ecclesiastes 10:8, the serpent bites when the hedges are broken. If we break the hedge, the enemy attacks. If we open the door to the enemy, he will restrict and slow down the process of God in our life. If we allow access to our heart, regardless of the situation, whatever God is bringing to us will begin to diminish, slow down, or possibly be aborted. Be careful.

For a few years in my life, I had a time of separation form the world. I separated myself while living in South Carolina near the Blue Ridge Mountains. For three and half years, I spent hours in prayer and fasting, seeking God constantly. In separation and hiding in God it brings forth the anointing. If we're hungry for an encounter with God, we will experience a time of separation in our life—separation from our family, friends, and the pure pleasures of life.

When I played the CDs with Bible verses, worship and warfare, it was a phenomenal time with consistent visitations. At the same time, I was receiving revelation, but there were also battles. Then there were great times of deliverance where God delivered me from everything of the world.

I remember one time, screaming at God to deliver me and I refused to get off the floor until I experienced Him. I said, "Until you deliver me from this _____, I am not moving from this spot." To show God how serious I was, I put on my best piece of clothing, got on my knees and ripped my garment. I tore my clothes like the priest would tear the sackcloth and lay on the ground.

Now that may not make sense to everyone, and the shirt may not have cost very much, but it was everything to me at that time. It was connected to me as something that I loved. Regardless of the monetary value, it showed the seriousness I was taking with God and He honored that.

On another occasion, I remember an experience in my kitchen where the hand of God, bigger than my body began to press hard against me, pressing me to the floor. I knew it was God's hand pushing and pressing me like olives. In order to get the oil out, the olives have to be crushed for the anointing to come forth. God was crushing me in order to use me.

4

SPIRITUAL DNA

*You made all the delicate, inner parts of my body and knit me
together in my mother's womb.*

(Psalm 139:13)

O NE OF THE THINGS I'VE LEARNED
from God when it comes to discovering
who I am and my identity in Christ is
determining what is my *spiritual DNA*. It is a wild
process figuring out who we really are. Every person
has to go through this progression in order to truly
be used by God at the level He intended for us. We
must figure out who we are and what is our spiritual

DNA. We discover it when we learn what moves us in the spirit.

When I first started reading the Bible, what I read did not always stick. It was slow at first, but the more I applied myself, I discovered that sometimes, a passage would jump off the page and I was amazed. Other times, nothing. Here is what I learned. There are certain scriptures that God will show to us that are for specific seasons of our life. At the time, it may not move us, but when we arrive in a different season, a passage will have a greater impact upon us. Be sensitive to those seasons.

We cannot become frustrated or discouraged when reading the Bible, especially when we feel like it is not working or we are not getting anything out of it. In due season, His Word will show up. When the Bible comes alive and we feel like a particular passage is for us, we cannot read it and then just move on to another passage.

When the scriptures come alive and a spark ignites in our spirit, it happens for a purpose. God is digging something within. It may be that God wants to bring deliverance, a healing, a miracle, or a revelation. So many variables can happen when the Word of God pierces the soul. Hebrews 4:12 (MB) says:

"For the word of God is alive and powerful.
It is sharper than the sharpest two-edged sword,
cutting between soul and spirit, between joint
and marrow. It exposes our innermost
thoughts and desires."

The Lord brings it to the surface but it is up to us to discern and figure out the purpose of that scripture. We have to pull on the anointing that flows from God's Word. We must meditate, focus, memorize and internalize the scriptures. We need to write it down, document our thoughts in categories so we don't have a bunch of confusing notes everywhere.

By organizing what God speaks to us when we study the Bible, we can better apply it to our life to further our process, and to accelerate what God is saying to us. If it is a scripture on love, then write a category labeled "love." If it is on scriptural warfare, write "warfare." Once we categorize it, we need to read it repeatedly. We must meditate on it as the Bible says in Joshua 1:8:

> *"Study this Book of Instruction continually.*
> *Meditate on it day and night so you will be sure*
> *to obey everything written in it. Only then will you*
> *prosper and succeed in all you do."*

On one occasion, I was in a situation and the Lord gave me this scripture in Psalm 34:10:

> *"The young lions do lack and suffer hunger;*
> *but they who seek the Lord shall not be in*
> *want of any good thing."*

I was in a season of financial drought and I did not know what to do. I knew that God had to help me. God had to deliver me. Only God could deal with my situation. So this scripture came to me, *they that seek the Lord shall not want any good thing*, and I knew that if I sought the Lord my answer would manifest. I shall not want any good thing.

What is a good thing? It is whatever we consider good. It is whatever we need.

My "good thing," at that moment, was I needed bills to be paid. I needed breakthroughs in specific areas. I needed finances to further projects. I sought the Lord; I shall not want any good thing, but my answer was not in praying for a breakthrough in that area. My answer was not in praying for financial increase, my answer was found when I dedicated 100% of my time to seek the Lord.

I sought God in prayer by focusing on Him. I sought the Lord with fasting. When I read the Word, I would look for Him. When I worshipped, I was seeking Him. I had no agenda. I had to learn to remove all my needs from the equation and completely set them to the side. That is a hard thing to do and is a test that every believer will go through.

There are all kinds of pressure in the natural realm that will try to push us to take our focus off Jesus. The enemy tries to get us to remove our eyes off Him. There will be times when we get distracted and we look at our natural circumstances. It was during these times I meditated, focused and pressed in until the manifestation happened.

As we read the Word, we must categorize what the Lord is doing in our life to discover who we are. We need to go through the whole Bible and write down every scripture that pops out. Some scriptures may pop out the first time around, while others on the second round. Every scripture that pops out carries a purpose. Now this purpose is going to determine our spiritual DNA. What do I mean by that?

I move in a realm of intense warfare. It's an authority that carries warfare power, and that's who I am. For me, God created me to be a deliverer, a Moses to this generation. God created me for that purpose. I am not moved on certain scriptures that somebody else may be moved on—though all those scriptures are great. It just doesn't spark something in me, because I carry a different purpose. I may have more scriptures that deal with warfare and deliverance than scriptures that deal with some other topic.

When we go through the Word, we will find everything we need that moves us.

Every believer has to learn to minister the Word. Not everyone is called to be a pastor, prophet or an apostle. We all have a purpose, but it may be different for each one of us. We are not all called to function in the same office. We are all called to minister God's Word whether it is to our coworkers, to our family, or to strangers.

If we try to learn something that really does not move us, we are forcing it. And if we force it, it is a lot harder to engrave it into our spiritual DNA. If it is not a part of us, it will cause us to miss our purpose. Purpose always defines who we are. Discovering who we are in Christ is what defines our spiritual DNA. When I discovered this, it was a game changer. It is what changes lives and it changed mine.

It is so important to figure out who we are and what's our purpose. When we do, it accelerates the process of our growth. This not only applies to the scriptures, but this also applies to worship. We have to figure out what sounds move us. Some sounds may move us that pertain to healing. When we find what moves us, it is the area we are called to and the area God wants us to minister with to others.

Particular sounds that move us into a dance, into praise or into warfare will define our purpose. There are so many different attributes available to us, but each of us has to figure out what helps us. What songs move us? Compile a list of songs that motivate the anointing of God. This all goes back to the previous chapter, setting the atmosphere.

If I play something that does not move me, what good is it? I need something that brings a divine awareness out of me in order to function the way God wants me to function.

I want it to move me. I want it to connect with me. I want it to bring that energy I need to find myself in Him. Everyone can develop their own playlist that they love. We need the songs that move us closer to God. When we find what moves us, we must learn it and then set the atmosphere by playing it. Set the atmosphere by living it, and watch the encounters increase with God's presence and power as His Spirit begins to manifest in your life.

5

PRAYER LIFE

But Jesus often withdrew to lonely places and prayed.
(Luke 5:16, NIV)

WHEN IT COMES TO AN ENCOUNTER with God, it is vital a believer understands the importance of the power of prayer. Without a prayer life, believers are powerless to the attacks of the enemy and void of God's presence. E.M. Bounds once said, "Preaching never edifies a prayerless soul."[1] Don't get me wrong. Going to church to hear a sermon, or

---

[1] *Power Through Prayer*, E. M. Bounds, Fleming H. Revell Company ©1920, reprinted by Baker Book House, p. 69.

listening to an inspired podcast message on YouTube is a needed ingredient to Christian growth. However, if that is all we do, we are missing opportunities for intimacy and an encounter with God.

Prayer is one of the secrets to power. Prayer is a key to unlocking access in the spirit realm, cultivating divine connections and relationships, along with developing an open communication with God. If we don't develop a prayer life we will never reach our potential or have an impact on others.

When I first started learning to pray, I would pray maybe one or two minutes if that, and if I prayed for five to ten minutes, I thought it was like a marathon. I actually thought I was praying for a long time. Then, when I developed a prayer language and combined prayer with speaking in tongues, time was no longer an issue.

Paul said something like this to the church at Corinth (1 Cor. 14:15):

"Well then, what shall I do? I will pray with
my spirit, and I will also pray with words I
understand; I will sing in the spirit,
and I will also sing in words I understand."

When we pray in the natural, time is limited. Praying in English (my native dialect) took a lot of effort. I am not saying that it cannot be done, but it seems more difficult at times to press in. However, when we pray in the spirit, it is different. It's like an engine that's revving. It's like throwing gasoline on a fire. When we pray in the spirit, it never gets old. It's never predicated on time nor do we get bored. We can go for hours and hours.

If we were to try to pray for hours in our natural language, we will struggle and possibly give up trying. We won't make it. There's just something about the spirit language that makes a difference.

When we go into prayer, we should do both—natural and spiritual languages. When we pray in the natural, we are limiting our understanding to our mind alone. But, when begin to speak in the spirit, our spirit receives the revelation and then it is transferred to our mind (psyche).

First Corinthians 2:13 says:

"When we tell you these things, we do not use words that come from human wisdom. Instead, we speak words given to us by the Spirit, using the Spirit's words to explain spiritual truths."

While in training for ministry, a pastor, where I was attending, asked me to lead the prayer session at the church. I submitted and said, "Yes." Suddenly, it hit me. *What am I going to say for a whole hour?* I had already agreed, so there was no backing out now. By now, my prayer language developed and I was praying for an hour. It not only came easy, but my prayers carried an anointing.

Each time I did so, I would feel great power like electricity and fire flowing into my body. When I prayed at the church, the people noticed something was upon me to lead with intercession. It came naturally.

We will only succeed in public because of what we do in private. I had to step out in faith and trust God to walk in a different dimension. God is faithful when we obey.

I went to the prayer session and began to lead prayer, not like a novice, but a seasoned warrior. Nevertheless, I was terrified for the first five or ten minutes. Then I relaxed, got into the spirit, didn't focus on the crowd and the power flowed. I just went at it and it was amazing. I had the confidence I needed to do this and from that moment forward, I led every prayer service. Besides leading prayer at the church, I started praying for an hour a couple times a week and I would pray for 30 minutes before the services.

I was in prayer a lot. It was good because it taught me to pray without ceasing. I wanted to go deeper. I pushed further and so one night, the pastor I was under told me to go for two hours. I thought, *two hours, what in the world? That's pushing it man, I don't know if I can do that.*

With the intensity I bring when I pray, I thought for sure I would lose my voice after an hour passed and be done. The first time I did a two-hour session, I felt accomplished and it felt amazing to go into the spirit realm with intercession.

When we come out of prayer, at that level, we feel so disconnected from the natural realm. The reality is—it feels different. That's because we're tapping into the spirit, praying in an unknown tongue and the natural surroundings around us just seem unreal. It is almost as if we're in the Matrix (the 1999 Hollywood blockbuster movie).

Now as my prayer life began to develop and I started to do this on my own to cultivate an atmosphere of prayer. I would find a solitude place and pray in secret to God. The Lord began to reward me for my sacrifice and the blessings started to flow.

From time to time, I would go to Minnesota to minister. I would drive from Florida to Minnesota, a 28-hour trip one-way. I did this about 20-30 times in ten years. It was a lot of driving and a lot of sacrifice. But I loved it, because I knew those 28 hours in a car would allow me time to focus on prayer and the Bible. It was as if it was just me and God.

The first time going to Minnesota, we were supposed to do three days of prayer, dealing with different topics. We knew that we would tap in for a lengthy time, but I had no clue how long it was going to be. As we were driving up, I got a call informing me that we were going to pray from 9 PM to 5 AM, eight hours.

I looked at my friend who was riding with me and said, "Are you kidding me? Eight hours?"

We arrived in Minnesota for the three-day prayer conference and I kicked it off. We took shifts. We started at 9 p.m. I did the first two hours and someone took the next two hours. Before we knew it, it was 5 a.m. It was so deep. To be in the spirit for nine hours of prayer was intense. When it ended, everyone wanted to leave to go home and rest. Not me, I wanted to continue for the presence of God was so strong.

We did 29 hours of prayer in three days, and then a 28-hour car ride, which was also filled with a lot of prayer. I spent more time in prayer in one week than most people do in ten years. The reality was this, God was raising me up for intercession. I was learning how to pray, how to tap into the realm of the spirit, how to do warfare, learning all the attributes of prayer, pushing past the flesh, and developing what would become a catalyst for my ministry.

I look back and remember when I could not pray for 10 to 15 minutes. I didn't think I could pray for an hour. Then, it was two hours, then a nine-hour prayer service.

Now I'm praying two to four hours a day. It is easy, because it comes naturally. Unless I'm spending two to four hours a day in prayer, in the Word and worship, I don't feel I've accomplished much in the day. That's a minimum now, and it's been increasing each month. God has been pushing me to do six to eight hours of consistent intercession. This activity has prepared me for what God is going to do in my life, my family, and my ministry.

One of the key secrets to an encounter with God is building a consistent prayer lifestyle.

Don't forget this: *a prayerless believer is a powerless believer.* If we don't live a lifestyle of prayer, we can never carry God's power. We see situations change in our life because it is a direct result of prayer.

6

TIME OF
SEPARATION

But when you pray, go into your room, close the door and pray to your Father, who is unseen. Then your Father, who sees what is done in secret, will reward you.

(Matthew 6:6, NIV)

WHAT ARE THE THINGS WE HAVE TO do in our spiritual walk to accomplish our purpose in life? How do we maintain a proper fellowship with God so the enemy cannot come in and distract us? The enemy is always going to come to kill, steal and destroy (John 10:10).

One of the secrets to Jesus' ministry and operating the way He did was His *times of separation*. He sought after solitude and silence, which is hard for many people, especially in the world we live in today. We live in a very fast-paced society, where people only care about getting things done as quickly as possible.

So many of us are in such a hurry to get things done, we neglect the very attributes of Jesus' life that led Him to obtain His success. He had breakthrough after breakthrough in His life. He ministered deliverance, healing, miracles, with signs and wonders. It was a byproduct of solitude, times of separation, isolating Himself to pray.

Most people these days cannot do that. Not that they cannot do it physically, they just do not discipline themselves enough to separate themselves from their day-to-day activity to be alone with God.

The Bible says in Psalm 46:10:

"Be still and know that I am God."

So many people cannot be still in an era of cell phones and the constant onslaught of entertainment at our fingertips. With all the new forms of entertainment, it is the most precious commodity we have. It is more valuable than gold, but people do not see that because deception has crept in.

I remember when cell phones first came out. They were not sophisticated devices. But today, they can be addicting. There has been many times when my cell phone has consumed me. Recognizing that this was the plan of the enemy to remove me from focusing on what really matters, I realized I had to shift my focus. No matter what happens in this world, if you do not adhere to the basic principles of what Christ did when He was on earth, you can never have an impact on people.

Jesus separated Himself to spend time alone to pray. He separated Himself to the mountains. He separated Himself beside the water. We too must separate ourselves and hide in God. It is a demand from the Father.

If we truly want to have an impact on this earth and a desire to be used by God, we have to make the most use with the time we have. We have to be aware that the human lifespan is not but a vapor. We are here one minute and gone the next.

If our main focus is how much impact we can have in this world, we have to centralize every activity, every word, and every action. If we spend all day watching TV, playing games on our phone, or just being consumed with nonsense, we will waste our life and never accomplish what God intended for us to do.

As we progress in technology, our day-to-day life becomes even more chaotic. It takes a strong-willed, strong-minded person to understand the basics of what I am writing. This principle will change our life no matter if we have flying cars or have all the technology of the Jetsons. It does not matter, maintaining the core principles of Christ will keep us in the perfect will of God. Mark 1:12,13 says:

"The Spirit then compelled Jesus to go into the wilderness, where he was tempted by Satan for forty days. He was out among the wild animals, and angels took care of him."

Think about it, we can have constant angelic encounters. It's going to be so amazing! However, in reality it is 40 days of temptation and 40 days of high-level demonic experiences. We can think, *we did not sign up for this God. This is not why we went into the fast.*

God taught me how to fast and when I started fasting, I had more attacks and more encounters in the demonic world than I did heavenly encounters. I mean 95% or more was bad. However, I was building a resume as I was breaking down my flesh in those fasts. I was gaining more authority and impact in the spirit realm. Demonic beings would confront me. But it was expected.

If we anticipate having an impact on this world, we will go face-to-face with the enemy. We will face temptation. The same was true with what Jesus faced in the wilderness.

The Bible says He was in the desert with the wild animals and angels attended Him. That was a place of loneliness. It was just Jesus and the Father, all the while being tempted of satan. He had to face a test in order to walk in dominion. But, when He came out of the wilderness, it says He came out in the power of the spirit. Mark 1:35 says:

"Very early in the morning while it was still dark,
Jesus got up left the house and went off
to a solitary place where he prayed."

The Jewish day started around 5 AM. The Bible says that He get up while it was still dark. Jesus spent many hours praying before the sun rose, as it states in Mark 2:13, 3:7 and 3:13:

"*Once again, Jesus went out beside the lake.*"

"*Jesus withdrew with his disciples to the lake in a large crowd from Galilee followed.*"

"*Jesus went out to the mountainside to pray and spent the night praying to God when morning came he called his disciples to him. When Jesus heard that John the Baptist had been beheaded he withdrew by boat privately to a solitary place.*"

One of the key things to take notice in this verse is to recognize that when we are in a place of emotional pain the world cannot give us comfort. We need to withdrawal privately to a solitary place, seek the Lord, seek the Father, seek the Holy Spirit and God will bring us comfort. Mark emphases in 6:16, 8:27:

> *"After Jesus had dismissed the crowd he went*
> *up on a mountainside by himself to pray.*
> *When evening came he was still there alone."*

> *"Once, when Jesus was praying in private,*
> *His disciples were with him he asked them,*
> *'Who do the crowds say I am?'"*

Understand that prayer is meant to be personal. There is nothing wrong with corporate prayer. It carries great power when two or three are gathered in His name and there is unity. Nevertheless, prayer is meant to be in oneness with God—a relationship in private. Jesus had great success, strength, compassion, wisdom, miracle-working power, and was able to deal with overwhelming demands and stress of ministry without becoming weighed down.

The problem with many ministers today is that they are so consumed with doing things so quickly, with a fast food or microwave mentality. They go through the motions in their ministry without much heart because they do not take time to separate themselves and just focus on God.

We all need to be alone to be strengthened and recharge our spiritual life. Ministry is war. It is a battle and a fight. We are contending every day for souls against satan, and because of the assignment, there's going to be counterattacks. There is going to be pressure and heaviness. All kinds of arrows will be fired at us if we do not maintain our solitude with God and separate ourselves.

Throughout the Scriptures, it consistently says Jesus separated Himself to seek the Father. Jesus' rich life of quiet prayer and intimacy was His source of love, wisdom and power. Jesus portrays a great rhythm of life in a wonderful metaphor. The sap from the vine flows into the branches and they bare clusters of juicy grapes. Jesus is the Vine, the Father is the gardener and the Holy Spirit is the life in the vine.

In John 15:1-15 Jesus taught us that we need to become as branches connected in a grapevine that is gardened by God. Jesus is explaining to us that the power to bear fruit for others comes from our intimate abiding in God. What Jesus taught, He lived. He only did what the Father showed Him.

When we abide in the Father's love, fruit will grow out naturally. It does not have to be forced out. It comes out without a struggle when we take time to separate ourselves from all the distractions of life to have a God encounter.

7

CALL TO THE MOUNTAIN

I lift up my eyes to the mountains—where does my help come from?

(Psalm 121:1, NIV)

THE BOOK OF PSALMS CONTAINS A SERIES of songs written by seven different worship leaders, including David, who wrote 73 of the 150 in our Bible. Naturally, the psalms give us insight into the heart of God and are beautiful poetic melodies that spark a flame conducive for worship and God encounters. So often, we read the psalms and miss their rich meaning. Conditioned to respond to our emotions, our perceived mind has a tendency to grasp only that which is currently happening on in our lives. In other words, our drama gets in the way of comprehending what the authors of Psalms were really trying to say.

Once I realized the importance of biblical meditation (Josh. 1:8,9), I began to read the psalms in a new light. I discovered there were hidden keys that are there and these are the three things that led me to an experience with God. One of the greatest experiences I ever had in my life was when I went to the mountain of God. I want to give the back-story, how I discovered specific keys that unlock doors to encountering God, first verified in Psalm15:1-5 (KJV):

"Lord, who shall abide in thy tabernacle?
who shall dwell in thy holy hill?
He that walketh uprightly, and worketh
righteousness,

and speaketh the truth in his heart.

He that backbiteth not with his tongue,

nor doeth evil to his neighbour,

nor taketh up a reproach against his neighbour.

In whose eyes a vile person is contemned;

but he honoureth them that fear the LORD.

He that sweareth to his own hurt, and changeth not.

He that putteth not out his money to usury,

nor taketh reward against the innocent.

He that doeth these things shall never be moved."

The powerful thing this Scripture tells us is that if we do the things we should, we will not be moved. What really caught my attention is at the beginning of the chapter, where it states: *"Who shall abide in the tabernacle? Who shall dwell in the holy hill?"*

I remember, as if it were yesterday, when God spoke to me saying, "I'm calling you to the mountain." When I heard that, it was like a cool breeze on a fall morning in South Carolina. The Bible says that the original couple, Adam and Eve, walked with God in the cool of the evening (Gen. 3:8). Now, the word "wind," in Hebrew is *ruach*, and can be translated, "breath," or "spirit." When God calls us to the "holy hill," He is waiting to meet us. However, in order for us to experience the breath of God and have an encounter, we must realize it is our responsibility to climb the mountain.

The first key I learned from the Psalms about climbing the mountain was to *press in*. In an attempt to process the word of the Lord, God began to share with me how people miss their encounters. The Lord showed me that in most worship services, the people are looking for God to touch *them*. But in reality, He wants them to touch *Him*. Immediately, when I heard that in my spirit, I thought of the woman with the issue of blood. She pressed through the crowd to touch the Lord. She came with an expectation to receive something—all she needed to do was touch the hem of His garment.

When she touched Jesus, the Bible says power left Him. When the Lord realized that virtue (energy) released from His body, He turned around and said, "Who touched me"? The puzzled disciples, said, "What do you mean Lord, who touched you"? How crazy? Everyone was touching Him. Jesus was walking through a mass audience of fans and the people were grabbing Him, as if He was a rock star. Surely, He felt the people pushing and pulling, but when this woman touched Him, it was different. She touched Him with expectation and faith.

Maybe this is why so many who attend church are not getting anything. They are waiting on God. They justify their meekness when quoting, *"Be **still** and know I am God,"* (Ps. 46:10, bold emphasis added). However, the Hebrew word for "still" does not mean to stop moving forward, but rather to relax or, "chill" in the midst of the journey. The woman with the issue of blood had a "be still and know I am God" encounter. It was her confidence, an expectation that created a new level of faith knowing her pursuit would bring her healing. But she received more!

The Bible says that Jesus told her, "Your faith has made you whole." Notice it does not say, "Your faith produced your healing." On the other hand, He did not say, "Your faith has brought you a miracle." We must catch this. When we enter worship, and we are waiting for Him *to come to us* to touch us, we may receive a miracle or a healing. But, when we pursue God, *when we chase Him*, we are made *whole*!

In my journey up the mountain, I started pushing my way in worship. I became a God chaser, pushing my way through the distractions, going into another realm of the spirit through prayer. With everything within me, I would seek (run after) the Lord. Here is the prerequisite. In Psalm 24, it says:

"The earth is the Lord's and the fullness thereof,
the world and they that were within,
for he has founded upon the seas
established upon the waters,
who shall ascend into the mountain of the Lord,
who shall stand in his holy place?
The one who has clean hands and a pure heart,
who does not trust in idols or swear by a false God,
they will receive blessing from the Lord
and vindication from God there savior,
such is the generation of those that seek him,
who seek your face, God of Jacob."

The second key is to purge our spirit from those things that so easily hold us back from an encounter. The Psalmist was saying, "he that has clean hands a pure heart, who have not lifted up his soul into vanity nor sworn deceitfully he shall receive the blessing from the Lord in righteousness from the God of his salvation." God is saying, the generation that seeks His face shall be able to ascend to the mountain of God. We shall be able to stand in His holy place, if we have clean hands and a pure heart.

I began to pray accordingly. "Lord, cleanse my hands, purify my heart. Help me not lift up my soul to vanity. Help me not to swear deceitfully." I renounced anything that would hold me back. With a pure heart, I begin to pray according to what Psalms 15 and 24 declared, "*Who can ascend the mountain of God*"? No one can just ascend God's mountain—God's holy hill and stand in a holy place without the prerequisites—expectation in the pursuit and faith in action.

✱ We must make ourselves available. That is why Moses went up the mountain. God's leader was a man of faith and he sought after God's presence. He climbed the mountain to have an encounter with God that produced the Ten Commandments. No one else was allowed to go up the mountain (Exod. 19, 20).

But unlike the children of Israel, we all have access to the mountain, which was made available through the New Covenant. We have the ability to access God with great dimensions, but only if we are willing to pay the price. Once on the mountain, we will engage with God. There we learn His voice. As we develop our relationship, we learn to follow the instruction of the Holy Spirit becoming sensitive to what grieves Him and pleases Him.

3. The third key is obedience. Obedience becomes a vital key that unlocks the doors to the spirit realm.

The Bible says, *"obedience is better than sacrifice,"* (1 Sam. 15:22). If the Lord is telling us not to do something—do not do it. Do not grieve the Spirit. If God tells us to do something, we must do it with no hesitation. Obedience strengthens our spirit, where as disobedience fuels our flesh.

To ascend the mountain, we must be prepared for the journey. Our level of obedience determines how successful we are in our climb. We must follow the pattern of Jesus when He said He only spoke what He heard the Father say; and He only did what He did after He saw what the Father showed Him.

Climb your mountain—press in, purify and obey His voice.

8

GUARD THE GATES

*They and their descendants were in charge of
guarding the gates of the house of the LORD—the house
called the tent of meeting.*

(1 Chronicles 9:13, NIV)

ONE OF THE MOST IMPORTANT THINGS
we can do as a believer, is guard the gates
that satan seeks to enter. If we break the
hedge the serpent bites, we defeat his devices. Satan
is always looking to access through sin, doubt and
unbelief. He does not care how he gets right of entry
to our soul, as long as he has access. One of the
main areas of our soul, which the enemy targets to

bring defilement to our life, is through our ears. What do we listen to? What sounds are we listening to? What are we allowing into our soul, shaping our mind, shaping our will, or shaping our emotions? What you listen to will either increase your spiritual antenna or cause static to block the air waves.

Satan also uses our eyes. What are we looking at? Are we looking at perverted things? Are we viewing things we should not be watching? Are we allowing entertainment, be it the TV or movies to defile us? Our eyes are the gateway to the soul. Our eyes are an open gate. The eyes are a window to the mind.

We can look into someone's eyes and see how much God they have inside by the light within their eyes. I believe there is a different glow about someone's eyes who is a committed believer. I can look at someone and instantly tell if they're a Christian or not and what level they are operating.

But, I can also look at somebody and tell if they are a seer or if they see in the spirit. I can tell because the light of Christ shines forth from their eyes.

The Bible says in Matthew 6:22; "*the eye is the lamp of the body.*" If our eye is clear, our whole body will be full of light. The eye is the lamp of the body, but if our vision is bad, the body also is full of darkness. Another great example is in Matthew 5:29, which says:

"*If your right eye makes you stumble tear it out and throw it from you, for it is better for you to lose one of your parts of your body than for your whole body to be thrown into hell.*"

Understand that satan seeks to access our life through our eyes. All sin falls under three areas: the lust of the eyes, the lust of the flesh and the pride of life.

In First John 2:16 it says:

"For everything in the world—the lust of the flesh, the lust of the eyes, and the pride of life—comes not from the Father but from the world."

The flesh lusts and it seeks to be empowered. What we see is whom we serve. If we feed our flesh, we serve our flesh. If we feed our spirit, then we will be led by the spirit.

The eye is one of the most targeted areas the enemy uses to infiltrate a believer's life.

Another area is the mouth. Satan uses the mouth as an entry point to access the soul. This is another gate that must be guarded. We cannot allow our mouth to be defiled and open the gate to sin. We have to be careful how our tongue speaks. The Bible says the tongue is a world of iniquity set on fire by, hell. We have to be cautious how we speak and the words we use.

The Bible says in Proverbs 18:21 (NIV),

"The tongue has the power of life and death, and those who love it will eat its fruit."

Another way satan attempts to destroy the soul is through sexual sin. Engaging in ungodly soul ties through sexual defilement will open the gate to sin and destruction. It will bring us into an arena where we are tormented in our mind, in our dreams and in our thoughts.

Remember all these gates give access to the soul. If our soul is completely turned over to the enemy, we are a casualty of war and cannot be used of God until there is deliverance in that area. This is why the Bible says in Proverbs 23:7 (KJV):

"As a man thinketh, so is he."

If satan can access our soul, our mind, our will and what we think, we are in bondage. If he can control our thoughts and shift our focus, we are doomed. That is the definition of witchcraft, being able to bend the will. Witchcraft targets the soul because if it can bend the will of an individual it puts them in a state of mind control.

The soul enters a place in the realm of the spirit where it is caged up by the enemy and tormented. That is why we can go through our daily life and not feel peace. We do not feel complete. We are tormented in our mind.

When tormented, our marriage can be under attack and our emotions out of control. The enemy consistently seeks to target our soul and that is where the struggle is. Our mind is the battlefield, which satan seeks to control and gain access to the soul. So, we must guard the gates.

9

RECOGNIZING OPEN HEAVENS

Oh, that you would burst from the heavens and come down!
How the mountains would quake in your presence!

(Isaiah 64:1)

ONE OF THE KEY SECRETS THAT I learned in my prayer walk was recognizing that my home carried a different atmosphere, like an open heaven when I prayed. When we hear the term, "open heaven" most believers think of an extended series of meetings called a revival. It is characterized by an unusual setting where various expressions of God's glory and power are manifested. For Charismatic's, an open heaven is accompanied by signs, wonders, healings and miracles. For Evangelicals, it is salvations and baptisms. But I believe an open heaven is a tangible evidence of heaven visiting earth with God's presence poured out upon a church, a community, a city, or a nation.

Advocates of the *open heaven* concept describe it as a season of supernatural blessings when revelation is abundant through God's prophets and apostles. It is a time when visitations are common, be it angels, prophetic words, dreams or an invasion of spiritual, physical and financial miracles.

Bill Johnson says, "an Open Heaven" is where there's a nearness of Heaven to earth. There's a sense of presence, there's a sense of clarity of thought of heart, and mind that is unusual. People think for themselves within an open heaven and are not influenced by the spirit of the day or the spirit that seems to have dominance in a certain geographical area."[1]

I believe God wants to pour out His Spirit upon *all* flesh. More lives can be transformed in one moment when we get under an open heaven. The more we spend time with God and in His presence, the more we want to stay there. The Bible says in Psalm 16:11:

> *"You make known to me the path of life;*
> *you will fill me with joy in your presence,*
> *with eternal pleasures at your right hand."*

We need to recognize where it is easiest to "tap in". For example, if we have a prayer closet (secret place) where we pray, we have saturated that atmosphere in prayer; thus, it can be so much easier

---

[1] https://bethelmusic.com/blog/open-heaven-bill-johnson/

to tap in to His presence when we are seeking God. Even if it is in a laundromat it can become a place where we pray while folding clothes. We should recognize where we are—not just in the natural, but in the spirit. We must understand that there are open portals and open heavens in specific areas— even laundromats. We carry the atmosphere of God inside us and wherever we choose to press into His presence, which becomes an open heaven.

If we can recognize that our connection, our flow in the spirit, can have a great impact in our lives, the more likely we are to press in to an open heaven. There is always going to be a location where we connect better, where God can meet us at in a different dimension.

Over a three to four year span, during my times of prayer and fasting, I remember having a very vivid dream about the wheel that Ezekiel saw. God showed me that wheel was in my front yard, in the area in which I prayed. It was a specific area that I was always drawn. When I walked around the house and prayed in this one spot, something kicked into overdrive. In Greek, it is called a *topos*, where we get the English word, "topographic," a specific area or region on a map." God has a topos for all of us.

When God showed me that, I started to discern that there was something different in this spot (topos), than there was anywhere else at my house. So, as I began to seek the Lord and press in, praying and fasting, Bible reading, meditation, whatever it may be; I found myself frequently visiting that spot. Then God told me this was an open heaven, an open portal in this location.

Later, God showed me another spot in my house where I connected deeper than I did in any other place of prayer. One of the ways to see this in operation in the Bible is looking at Jacob's ladder in Genesis 28 verse 10-12; 16-17:

> *"As is Jacob left Beersheba and set out for*
> *Haran, he reached a certain place, where he*
> *stopped for the night because the sun had set.*
> *Taking one of the stones there he put it under his*
> *head and lay down to sleep. He had a dream in*
> *which he saw a stairway resting on the earth with*
> *its top reaching to heaven and the angels of God*
> *were ascending and descending on it.*
> *There above it stood the Lord; and he said*
> *I am the Lord and the God of your Abraham*
> *and God of Isaac; I will give you and your*
> *descendents the land of which you are lying.*
> *When Jacob awoke from his sleep,*
> *he thought surely the Lord is in this place*
> *and I'm not aware of it. He was afraid and said,*
> *'How awesome is this place, this is none*

other than the house of God,

the very gate of heaven.'"

This is the gate of heaven. It is a specific place where a portal opened up and he saw the angels going up and down. Now Jesus, when He was in Jerusalem, He spent most of His time at the Mount of Olives, His usual spot of prayer. Why? It was an open heaven for Him. Something established a connection in the spirit realm as He began to pray. It was a location where angels descended, and ministered to Him where He sweat drops of blood.

Think of it, finding our open heaven will sustain us in the middle of our greatest attack. It is there we find access to heaven's power and demonstrate victory in every area of our lives!

10

MAKE IT HAPPEN

*The smallest of them will become a family. The weakest of them
will become like a mighty nation. At the right time I,
the LORD, will make it happen quickly.*

(Isaiah 60:22, God's Word Translation)

I HAVE LEARNED THROUGH MY EXPERIENCES that the secrets to an encounter with God are something every believer has access. They are the keys to unlock deeper dimensions for access to God. It is like a code that unlocks a believer to a deeper dimension for a stronger walk in the Lord.

But in order for an encounter, something beyond our normal prayer time, we need to make it happen. Going deeper into the spirit realm and experiencing something fresh takes effort. Going from the outer court, to the inner court takes preparation, meditation and dedication.

My journey begins in a worship service. As I am on the platform worshiping, I hear the Lord call in the spirit and say, "Come to the mountain." *What does that mean?* I thought. Usually when God speaks to me, it appears in mysteries or parables and with that, discernment is necessary. Sometimes when a divine download takes place, it takes time to unravel the exact mystery of what God is trying to reveal to me.

I look at the crowd and everyone is worshipping. Maybe a thousand people in attendance and in the middle of worship, God tells me to look at the people. As I watch and observe, God says that everybody here is expecting Me to touch them, when in reality; I am waiting on the people to pursue Me. Pursuit is proof of passion. Whatever we are passionate for will direct our decisions, determine our friends, and direct our path.

Immediately, as I wrote in chapter seven, I see in my spirit the narrative of the woman with the issue of blood. I picture her pressing through the crowd. She touches the Lord. Then, it hits me—we must seek the Lord while He may be found.

The revelation comes to me repeatedly all that month. Like this woman who pressed through the crowds to touch Jesus, I knew that God wanted me to do the same. So, I began to press in and go deeper with every part of my being. I was pursuing God like never before. I was not going to sit back and wait for God to touch me.

The actions of this diseased woman could have got her killed. She was unclean. According to Mosaic

Law, a person with her condition was not permitted in a crowd less she transmits her disease. In addition, if she touched a priest or a member of the religious system, she could be stoned. However, nothing was going to prevent her from becoming whole. Many touched Jesus that day, but only one received virtue. Her pursuit, her determination, her faith, and her drive, even caught Jesus off guard. Thus, His response was, "Who touched me"?

As I gazed over the audience that night, my view is so clear from the platform. I could see the crowd worshipping, but not pressing in. With hands lifted up and tears running down their face, they were waiting for an encounter and not climbing a mountain. They were waiting for God to come to them, when He was asking them to come to Him. When we decide that we are going to pursue Him, then we can be made whole.

I digested that revelation and I began to push hard into worship. I could feel a portal opening in the spirit realm. A different dimension had been unlocked within me. I cannot adequately describe it, but I sensed boldness and, in the spirit, there was presented to me a right of entry.

A few days later, I am lying in bed, taken in the spirit, very different from a dream or a vision. I mean, literally I am out of my body into another dimension, in another realm, transported into my grandmother's old house. Sounds crazy, I agree—not something we are taught in a mid-week Bible study.

My intensive pursuit permitted me to experience something brand new, something supernatural, and something extraordinary compared to my prayer life before this encounter.

It is important to know that when we are taken in the spirit, we must decipher what we are about to engage, such as, spiritual warfare or an angelic visitation. I felt in my spirit I was about to go into a battle. In this case, I was at my grandmother's house and this was not good.

I see a long tunnel that stretched from her house into outer space. I see this tunnel and I know I need to go in it. I see a blinking of light. I jump into the tunnel and the journey begins. It was like, when you go to a bank drive thru and make a deposit, placing the documents and/or funds into a container, and when engaged, it shoots through a tube to the teller's location. This is the best description I can give to explain what it felt like when I was transported. It was like my body perfectly fit into a tunnel and I was shot up at the speed of light.

When I shot up through the tunnel, it was allied with demons. As I was flying through the tunnel and their claws were grabbing for me. I knew in my heart if I feared that if even one claw touched me, I would instantly drop back and lose the experience. In my heart, I purposed not to stop until I pressed through.

I pressed into that encounter and I was out on the other side. I am floating in space in the spirit and when I looked at a distance, I could see a massive ball of light like the size of the earth. It is covered in lightning and electricity. I can hear the deep static popping all around it.

I said to myself, *what in the world is that* and the moment I did, I begin to move toward it at the speed of thought. I begin to get pushed toward the ball of light, a massive globe, and I was probably the size of an ant. I stick my hand out to touch it and immediately, I am electrocuted worse than any power source that I could ever endure in the natural realm. I thought I was going to die. The electricity was so powerful. It drew me back.

Living in a rural area or camping in the woods or the mountains, the stars are visible and you can easily see the lightning light up the skies. Any time it's lightning, it's like flash photography. For a split second, we are able to see everything in the sky.

There was a flash of light and I was able to see what I touched, what appeared to be the eye of God! I was standing before the Creator. He had white hair, a crown, and massive eyes full of lightning. I cry out in awe of the majesty of God. I fall back to earth in my body and land back into my grandmother's house, lying on the floor. I look at myself and I am covered in an amber tinted film, like a mist—the glory is all over me.

The word "glory" in Hebrew means weight. That weight implies an influence or impression. To be "covered in glory" means God stamps His weight, His influence or impression on our life. We are to increase "from glory to glory," and to do so, we must separate ourselves for worship, meditation, reading and studying scripture, and to have a lifestyle of prayer and fasting.

By applying the principles expressed in this book, they will assist us as the gateway to an open heaven. God wants to share His kingdom in our lives. We cannot continue at the same level. We must go higher. We must go deeper. We must never give up until we reach the level God intended us to live. In order for us to walk in our full potential, we need to make it happen!

Get ready for a heavenly lifestyle by applying the secrets to an encounter with God!

About the Author

Joshua Giles is an apostolic and prophetic visionary, author, leader, entrepreneur and a business consultant. He is passionate for souls, discipleship, worship and God's presence.

Josh's prophetic insight and gift of intercession has been used to bring an "open heaven" in several different evangelistic and pastoral ministries. His fresh revelation imparts a special anointing that activates spiritual gifts, breaking bondages and setting the captives free. He travels nationally and internationally in crusades and TV outlets around the world.